DEEPLY *ROOTED*

STORIES OF LIVES ROOTED IN SCRIPTURE

DR. JOHN AND KELLY CHESNUT
WITH MELISSA PAREDES

Deeply Rooted

ISBN 978-0-938978-45-9

Published in the United States of America

Editor in Chief: Melissa Paredes

Editor: Jennifer Stasak

Designer: Phoebe Thomas, with Anna Broussard-Johnson

Producers: Vicky Mixson, Kristie Frieze, and Kathy Zoetewey

To learn more about Bible translation, visit **wycliffe.org**.

To order copies of the book, visit **shop.wycliffe.org**.

TABLE OF CONTENTS

DAY 1

GROWING DEEP ROOTS

I pray that from his glorious, unlimited resources he will empower you with inner strength through his Spirit. Then Christ will make his home in your hearts as you trust in him. Your roots will grow down into God's love and keep you strong. And may you have the power to understand, as all God's people should, how wide, how long, how high, and how deep his love is. May you experience the love of Christ, though it is too great to understand fully. Then you will be made complete with all the fullness of life and power that comes from God.
—Ephesians 3:16-19

Paul's words in Ephesians 3 are a favorite of mine (Kelly). I am passionate about praying Scripture over people and situations. After all, Scripture is God's very own words, so praying them back to him is not only edifying to my soul but also honoring to him!

I'm also a lover of words because they paint pictures in my mind's eye that inspire me mentally, emotionally, and spiritually. Paul's words in his epistles paint great pictures for all of us, don't you think?

Painting pictures across languages and cultures can be a little complicated though. Each culture is unique and the context for understanding changes. For instance, how do you explain the phrase "lamb of God" to a culture in an area of the world where there aren't any sheep? Or how do you explain the biblical phrase "white as snow" in a culture where the closest thing to snow might be miles of white glistening sand?

That's why Wycliffe Bible Translators exists—so that people can have access to God's Word in a language and format they clearly understand. We're passionate about seeing people all around the world have the opportunity to meet God through Scripture, to know God through his Word, and to grow deep roots because they are able to understand "how wide, how long, how high, and how deep his love is" (Eph. 3:18b) for themselves.

In the following days, you'll hear stories from around the world of lives that are transformed by the power of Scripture. You'll read about generations of families who are—or will be—impacted when they read, listen to, or watch the Bible in their language. Without access to God's Word, we can't grow deep roots in our spiritual lives; we can only float like a tumbleweed in the desert winds.

Before we dive into stories of impact, I want to pray Ephesians 3:16-19 over you and over the millions of people around the world who are still waiting to have access to God's life-giving Word so that they too can understand how great God's love is for them:

> I pray that from his glorious, unlimited resources he will empower you with inner strength through his Spirit. Then Christ will make his home in your hearts as you trust in him. Your roots will grow down into God's love and keep you strong. And may you have the power to understand, as all God's people should, how wide, how long, how high, and how deep his love is. May you experience the love of Christ, though it is too great to understand fully. Then you will be made

> complete with all the fullness of life and power that comes from God.

Amen, Lord Jesus! Make us complete in you.

SOWING SEEDS

If you're someone who is richly blessed to have God's Word in your language, stop and pray Ephesians 3:16-19 over people who are still waiting for Scripture so that they might have the opportunity to grow their roots down into God's love.

FOR MILLIONS OF PEOPLE
AROUND THE WORLD,
SCRIPTURE IN THEIR
LANGUAGE LOOKS LIKE THIS:

DAY 2

LOVE GOD, LOVE PEOPLE

"The most important commandment is this: 'Listen, O Israel! The Lord our God is the one and only Lord. And you must love the Lord your God with all your heart, all your soul, all your mind, and all your strength.' The second is equally important: 'Love your neighbor as yourself.' No other commandment is greater than these." —Mark 12:29-31

When I (John) was growing up, my dad had a rule whenever we bought something that needed to be assembled or operated for the first time: Always read the instructions.

When I was fifteen, we bought a barbecue with a fancy self-igniting system. Dad said I could assemble it. The instructions were complicated. I read and re-read the booklet. Finally, I decided that at my mature age, there were few things in life that I couldn't figure out on my own. I assembled the barbecue without instructions.

Upon attempting to ignite the grill with the auto-igniter and failing to make it work, I decided to simply throw a match into the barbecue. It lit! And the resulting fireball instantly removed the hair from my hands, arms, eyelashes, and eyebrows.

At times, we attempt to operate our own lives without consulting the instruction manual—God's Word. Like my near-death experience lighting the grill, things often don't turn out so well.

One day as Christ was talking to some religious leaders, one asked, “Of all the commandments, which one is the most important?” Jesus replied, “The most important commandment is this: ‘Listen, O Israel! The Lord our God is the one and only Lord. And you must love the Lord your God with all your heart, all your soul, all your mind, and all your strength.’ The second is equally important: ‘Love your neighbor as yourself.’ No other commandment is greater than these” (Mk. 12:28b-31).

I love how Christ was explicit in his response. Unlike human instruction manuals, he was clear. If you and I desire to honor God through our obedience, we need to love him and love people. This truth is simple to understand but takes a lifetime to institute.

There are nineteen different words for “love” throughout Scripture. It’s used as a noun, adjective, and verb. When used in reference to God, it’s a noun—it’s who he is. “God is love” (1 Jn. 4:8-16). It’s the very nature of his character.

When used as an adjective, it describes us as seen in our actions toward God and others. Used as a verb, it describes the action taken or to be taken, be it past, present, or future. And it’s often an imperative—a command—to love God and people.

When the word “love” is used as a command, the underlying implication is that love is also a choice—a choice to respond in obedience or not.

Our love for God and people flows from being deeply rooted in knowing God, abiding in Christ, and growing in grace and Christlikeness. Only then can we live out Jesus’s command to love God and love people.

SOWING SEEDS

Jesus calls us to love God and to love people. How can you choose to love God and love people today?

God showed how much he loved us by sending his one and only Son into the world so that we might have eternal life through him. This is real love—not that we loved God, but that he loved us and sent his Son as a sacrifice to take away our sins. Dear friends, since God loved us that much, we surely ought to love each other. No one has ever seen God. But if we love each other, God lives in us, and his love is brought to full expression in us.
—1 John 4:9-12

DAY 3

GOD SO *DVU'D* THE WORLD

"For this is how God loved the world: He gave his one and only Son, so that everyone who believes in him will not perish but have eternal life." —John 3:16

"Love" is an overused word in the English language, don't you think? We apply it to so many things: chocolate, exercise, family. We love all of these things conditionally based on our preferences, perspectives, or even our emotions on that particular day! But have you ever imagined what it might be like if you spoke a language that didn't have a word that was the equivalent of the "unconditional love" God has for us?

That's exactly what happened for the Hdi people of Cameroon. One night in a dream, God prompted translator Lee Bramlett to look at the Hdi word for love. Lee and his wife, Tammi, had learned that verbs in Hdi consistently end in one of three vowels: -i, -a, and -u. But when it came to the word for love, they could only find -i and -a. Why no -u?

Lee asked the translation committee, "Could you *dvi* your wife?" They responded, "Yes." That would mean that the wife had been loved but the love was gone.

So then Lee asked, "Could you *dva* your wife?" Again they said yes; that kind of love depended on the wife's actions. She would be loved as long as she remained faithful and cared for her husband well.

Then Lee prompted: “Could you *dvu* your wife?” Everyone laughed. “Of course not!” they said. “If you said that, you would have to keep loving your wife no matter what she did, even if she never got you water, never made you meals. Even if she committed adultery, you would be compelled to just keep on loving her. No, we would never say dvu. It just doesn’t exist.”

Lee sat quietly for a while, thinking about John 3:16, and then he asked, “Could God dvu people?”

There was complete silence for a few minutes; then tears started to trickle down the weathered faces of these elderly men. Finally they responded.

“Do you know what this would mean?” they asked. “This would mean that God kept loving us over and over, millennia after millennia, while all that time we rejected his great love. He is compelled to love us, even though we have sinned more than any people.”

One simple vowel, and the meaning was changed from, “I love you based on what you do and who you are” to, “I love you based on who I am. I love you because of me and not because of you.”

God had encoded the story of his unconditional love right into their language. For centuries, the little word was there—unused but available, grammatically correct and quite understandable. When the word was finally spoken, it made them question their entire belief system. If God was like that, and not a mean and scary spirit, did they need the spirits of the ancestors to intercede for them? Did they need sorcery to relate to the spirits? Many decided the answer was no, and the number of Christ followers quickly grew from a few hundred to several thousand.

The New Testament in Hdi is available for more than fifty thousand speakers who can now understand the unconditional love that God displayed when he sent Jesus, his one and only Son, to earth.

Do you remember the first time you read or heard John 3:16 and learned about God's love for you? God's Word is translated around the world, people are gaining access to this great love story in their own language. The cross changes everything! Someday, the last word of the last bit of Scripture for the last community will be done, and everyone will be able to understand the story of God's unconditional love.

SOWING SEEDS

There are almost three hundred languages spoken in Cameroon. Translation work is ongoing across the country. Pray that one day, all languages in Cameroon would be able to understand John 3:16 for themselves!

Ɗvuɗva Lazglafta ta ghəŋa
haɗik, kəl tsi ka vlatá Zwaŋani
turtuktuk, dər wa ta zlghafta,
zwaɗuta a wu, mutsafmutsa
ta hafu ŋa kɗekedzeŋ.
Yuh 3:16
(John 3:16 in Hdi)

DAY 4

LOVE GOD WITH ALL YOUR HEART

The man answered, "You must love the Lord your God with all your heart, all your soul, all your strength, and all your mind.' And, 'Love your neighbor as yourself.'"
—Luke 10:27

What does Scripture tell us about loving God with all our hearts?

We're first encouraged to love God with all our hearts in Deuteronomy 6:5, which says: "And you must love the Lord your God with all your heart, all your soul, and all your strength." In this verse, the Hebrew word for "heart" is similar in meaning to the Greek word used in Mark 12:30. In that verse, Strong's Concordance defines the "heart" as "the center and seat of spiritual life. [It's] the soul or mind, as it's the fountain and seat of the thoughts, passions, desires, appetites, affections, purposes, endeavors; of the will and character."

In Western cultures, the heart is viewed as the seat of our emotions. That's why we say things like, "I love you with all my heart." But did you know that for other cultures around the world, the heart isn't necessarily the organ they attach emotions to?

In Papua New Guinea, the Awa people think of the liver as their center, while the Rawa people think of the stomach as their center!

But Scripture indicates that the heart is so much more than the sum of our feelings; it's a reflection of who we really are (Prv. 27:19). Scripture is filled with verses that speak to the condition of our hearts and its correlation to our actions. Proverbs 4:23 says, "Guard your heart above all else, for it determines the course of your life."

The book of Proverbs is a collection of wise adages and principles by which to live. It was written by Israel's third king, Solomon. At the beginning of King Solomon's reign, God appeared to him in a dream and said: "What do you want? Ask, and I will give it to you!" (1 Kgs. 3:5) Solomon replied with a request for God: "'Give me an understanding heart so that I can govern your people well and know the difference between right and wrong. For who by himself is able to govern this great people of yours?' The Lord was pleased that Solomon had asked for wisdom" (1 Kgs. 3:9-10).

Much of Proverbs concerns the condition of the heart. Throughout the book, the word for heart appears ninety-one times as the Hebrew noun *leb*, referring to the inner man—that which makes up the mind, will, understanding, heart, and soul. Leb is also considered the seat of appetites, emotions and passions, and courage. Interestingly enough, in some of Solomon's proverbs, leb is also translated as the word for "wisdom" or "understanding."

In Proverbs 4, Solomon shares fatherly wisdom for pursuing a godly life. The admonishment to guard one's heart "above all else" (v. 23) is the key to staying the course. It is the key to maintaining pure thoughts, words, actions, intents, and motivations. The everyday choices we make influence the direction our lives take. Guarding our hearts means choosing Christ over sin and self—every time.

SOWING SEEDS

Papua New Guinea is one of fourteen countries in the Pacific, and home to nearly nine hundred languages—more than ten percent of all the world's languages! Papua New Guinea is made up of more than six hundred islands, which adds to the language diversity in this country. Pray that more people, like the Awa and Rawa, would be able to understand God's love in their heart—or their liver and stomach too!

DAY 5

HEAD VS. HEART

For it is by believing in your heart that you are made right with God, and it is by openly declaring your faith that you are saved. —*Romans 10:10*

Before joining Wycliffe Bible Translators back in 2001, Kelly and I (John) served as church planters in the greater Denver area. Together we served in a variety of roles over the years—first I served as a youth pastor and then executive pastor, and Kelly as the worship leader. During our younger years of marriage we invested a lot of time and energy into the church's youth, wanting to equip disciples who were passionate about God and his Word.

We also had the privilege of leading international missions trips—to Mexico, Brazil, and China—that helped cast vision for the need of the global church to continue to advance. It was in this season that we came face-to-face with the reality that without God's Word in their language, it's very difficult for the church to truly grow and to successfully develop deep roots. That's why Bible translation is so important, and what ultimately drew us to Wycliffe as God laid on our hearts the importance of this foundational component of church growth.

In April 2019, the Giryama people of Southeast Kenya finally celebrated the complete Bible in their language—after a century of waiting! About two thousand people in traditional dress celebrated the long-awaited event, dedicating their Bible to the glory of God. The festive ceremony featured singing and dancing and attracted the presence of church leaders as well as many local and national political leaders.

Bishop Mika Kenga, who is more than one hundred years old, trembled as he cried out in praise to God for allowing him the privilege of being able to hold the Giryama Bible in his hands. Many of the men and women who had tirelessly helped translate the New and Old Testaments died before the entire Bible was completed. But their painstaking efforts were not in vain!

Joseph S. Ngowa—one of the translators and a member of the dedication planning committee—acknowledged those early pioneers and said: "I salute those men and women of God who worked tirelessly to see this work come to completion. I believe their souls [are rejoicing], seeing what they prayed and labored for has been completed. To me, this [is] the second greatest thing that the Lord [has] done for the Giryama people apart from saving them."

Peter Munguti, a pastor among the Giryama, shared: "We have seen the church getting the passion for wanting to see God's people receive God's Word in their language in Kenya. If you speak to a man in a foreign language, that goes to his head. But if you speak to that same man in their language [that they can understand], it goes to his heart."

I don't know about you, but it's all too easy for me to take for granted the fact that I've always had access to God's Word in a language that speaks to both my head and my heart. But when faced with the realization that millions of people around the world don't have access to Scripture—perhaps even in a language that only speaks to their head, let alone their heart!—we couldn't sit idly by. We wanted to engage with and be a part of this life-transforming work.

One day we'll be able to rejoice in heaven with our Giryama brothers and sisters, and communities just like this, knowing that because they had Scripture in their language, they were able to believe in their hearts that Jesus is Lord. That is truly the foundation for the roots of faith that we grow as we learn the heart and character of God through his Word.

SOWING SEEDS

YouVersion is a partner of Wycliffe Bible Translators and hosts more than 1,750 languages on the Bible app and **bible.com**. Take a few minutes to go there and look up your favorite verse in another language. Pray for that community, and then pray for the communities around the world who are still waiting for even one verse of Scripture in their language.

Kwani mut'u akuluhira na moyowe akahendywa muhachi, na akanena kwa kanwake mwenye akaokoka.

Arumi 10:10

(Romans 10:10 in Giryama)

DAY 6

WAFFLES

The eyes of the Lord search the whole earth in order to strengthen those whose hearts are fully committed to him. —2 Chronicles 16:9

We enjoy a tradition of sharing Sunday morning waffles with our grandchildren. It's something they look forward to and we look forward to sharing it with them.

Waffles have a grid-like pattern of "boxes." Some waffles have shallow boxes while others (like the Belgian waffles our grandchildren enjoy) are deeper. Our grandchildren love to fill their Belgian waffles with fresh strawberries and whipped cream—the more, the better. And Belgian waffles have the space to fill each and every square!

We can create mental boxes just like waffles as a way to keep track of things in our lives. We make a box for work, one for ministry, another for church, and one for relationships. Each compartment takes up space in our minds. It helps us organize our time, focus, and effort.

But we also tend to do the same thing with our hearts.

Jesus calls us to love God with all of our hearts. Yet our ability to compartmentalize things is harmful. We're called to have undivided hearts: hearts that love God in every area and every way.

So what do undivided hearts look like? Undivided hearts are willing to love God and give him access to every part of our lives, not just our work or ministry. Our leisure time is fully his. The shows we watch on television and the books we read belong to him. The thoughts we have about other people belong to him—and when those thoughts don't reflect the heart of God, we must realign them with his truth, love, and grace because they are his.

Everything we say, do, or think is rooted in our hearts (Lk. 6:45). A heart that is wholly the Lord's is one that produces good fruit in all areas of life—not just the seemingly "spiritual" aspects.

As believers, everything we're about is spiritual. There is no differentiation, no compartmentalization, because all that we do is to be done with the intent of honoring and glorifying God. Whether in our jobs, our conversations with non-Christian friends and family, our grocery store trips, our school car line pick-ups, or our time spent on social media—all things should reflect hearts that are fully committed to God. To remember this and live it out is to love God wholeheartedly.

SOWING SEEDS

Take some time to pray and ask God to reveal what parts of your life you haven't fully surrendered to him. Make it an intentional habit to find ways to integrate Jesus into your daily tasks as you strive to have a heart that's fully committed to him.

DAY 7

LOVE GOD WITH ALL YOUR SOUL

Bless the Lord, O my soul;
And all that is within me, bless his holy name!
—Psalm 103:1 (NKJV)

More often than not, the word for "soul" throughout Scripture is defined as "the seat of our emotions, desires, affections and aversions—the part of us that feels, thinks, and decides, involving our mind, will, and character."

Our soul is what unites the various parts of our wills, minds, and bodies together into a single life. It's a life that's completely, entirely, absolutely, wholeheartedly designed to connect with God. Psalm 103:1 says: "Bless the Lord, O my soul; And all that is within me, bless his holy name!" (NKJV).

David wrote this beautiful psalm of devotion and praise. In *The Treasury of David, Volume 4*, Charles H. Spurgeon writes, "We should attribute [Psalm 103] to his later years when he had a higher sense of the preciousness of pardon, because a keener sense of sin, than in his younger days."

The God who forgives, heals, redeems, crowns, and satisfies is filled with tender compassion, mercy, and love toward those who fear him. As David writes in Psalm 103:2: "Bless the Lord, O my soul, and forget not all his benefits" (NASB). The word "bless" means "to kneel." It's the same Hebrew word used in Psalm 95:6: "O come, let us worship and bow down: let us kneel before the LORD our maker."

Our souls are called to bow in submission to the Creator. Our lives—all that is within us—kneel in worship and praise as we seek to love and obey God with all our hearts and all our souls. As we grow in our relationship with God, he creates hearts that long to obey him. Our obedience is no longer something we "have to do" but rather a reflection of what we want to do because of who we are—dearly loved children of God. Our souls become more and more at rest as we daily abide in Christ, remembering who we are in Christ and walking in obedience as we align every part of our lives with God.

That phrase—"in Christ"—is critical to our understanding of what it means to walk in obedience.

When the Aitape West Cluster translators in Papua New Guinea began working on the book of 1 John, they struggled to describe the believer's intimate union with Christ as it is expressed in the phrase "in Christ." The cluster languages only use the word "in" literally, to convey the physical placement of one object inside another.

After reflection, the translators found a way to communicate this crucial idea, saying that believers are "really fastened or stuck" to Jesus, in the same way that a lizard is firmly stuck to a tree.

Our prayer is that you will be "really fastened or stuck" to Jesus, so that your love for him pours forth from a soul that is truly rooted in Christ.

SOWING SEEDS

It can be easy to allow our emotions to lead us, rather than us leading our emotions—especially in today's world, where culture tells us the lie that our life's goal should be to make ourselves happy. What does it look like to be so rooted in Jesus that our faith comes not from our emotions, but from the knowledge of who God is and who we are in him?

DAY 8

BUILDING A LIFE

And now, just as you accepted Christ Jesus as your Lord, you must continue to follow him. Let your roots grow down into him, and let your lives be built on him. Then your faith will grow strong in the truth you were taught, and you will overflow with thankfulness.
—Colossians 2:6-7

With the last name of "Chesnut," you can imagine the jokes and comments that are made to me (Kelly). I recall even on our honeymoon (which was in May, by the way), someone singing, "Chestnuts roasting on an open fire" to us. As a new wife, I was still in the moony stage of taking on my new name. Flash forward more than thirty years later, and John and I still get that song sung to us every holiday season!

This got me thinking about chestnut trees and the roots they grow. I learned that many nut trees—including chestnut trees—have just one main root, almost like a skinny carrot. This main root needs to be planted in a hole that's wide and deep so that it can grow well. The tree needs fertile soil for good growth, with lots of nutrients and water in order for it to thrive.

The same is true in our relationship with Jesus. We need to be able to grow deep roots in him, building our lives in the rich soil of his Word. But what happens in seasons when it feels like growth is hard?

Teresia is an elderly lady from the Marakwet community in Kenya who often holds a personal worship service every Sunday outside her house.

One day, Reverend Paul Kanda, a translator from the community, decided to visit her. During their time together, Rev. Kanda realized that it was difficult for Teresia to attend the usual Sunday services due to her failing health.

So Rev. Kanda gifted Teresia the Marakwet audio Bible. Teresia was thrilled and said that listening to the audio Bible made her feel like she was attending church every day! It was like her pastor was speaking directly to her.

Since then, other elderly Marakwet ladies from her neighborhood joined Teresia and now all listen to the audio Bible at Sunday services outside her home!

And this group isn't the only one impacted by access to Scripture. "The hunger and thirst for the Scriptures is evident," a project adviser said. "Christians have, time and again, reiterated that their joy will be complete when they hold the full Marakwet Bible in their hands."

Janet and Thomas are blind, but they attended a showing of the *JESUS* film in Marakwet. The next day, Janet narrated the whole story—as if she was seeing what was going on in the film!

Thomas shared, "Today I was able to hear and understand the story of Jesus so [much better] than ever before. If those of us who are blind can hear and understand it without seeing, how about those who can hear and see what was going on in the film? You will never have any excuse during the judgment day of Christ."

Neither Teresia's failing health nor Janet and Thomas's blindness hindered them from actively nurturing the soil of their relationship with Jesus. Even when obstacles stood in their way, they still intentionally built their lives on Jesus—what a testament of God's hand at work!

I cannot wait for the day when I get to meet Teresia, Janet, and Thomas and rejoice with them that they not only chose to follow Jesus, but also sought to build their life on him. And as a result of their decision, who knows how many other lives will be changed for God's glory! Their roots are a testament to their communities that God is their source of hope and their true foundation.

SOWING SEEDS

Growing our roots in Jesus and building our lives upon him requires intentionality—not just on a personal level, but also as a legacy to pass on in your family or even your community. Reflect on the spiritual legacy you're currently creating, and pray for people like Teresia, Janet, and Thomas who are also changing the narrative of their family and community's spiritual legacy as they root themselves in Scripture.

DAY 9

BECOMING ONE WITH JESUS

"I am the vine; you are the branches. Whoever abides in me and I in him, he it is that bears much fruit, for apart from me you can do nothing." —John 15:5 (ESV)

My family says that I (Kelly) don't have a green thumb, but rather a black thumb. I've been told plants need to be prepared to survive extreme drought conditions or flash flooding when they enter my home. I somehow even managed to kill a cactus! John has told me for years that he can hear the despairing screams of plants as they're brought into our house, knowing that they're about to meet their demise.

While we laugh about my propensity to kill plants, I'm reminded about when Jesus told his disciples in John 15 that he is the vine, and we are the branches. We bear fruit when we consistently abide in him, but apart from him, we can do nothing.

Paulo Kijuu is a Bible translator for the Rangi language of Tanzania. When the team worked on the John 15 passage with their translation consultant, they talked about what it means to abide in Jesus. "I have heard John 15:5 many times in Swahili and in English," said Paulo. "A branch of a vine cannot 'live in' the vine. Instead it is 'attached' or connected to the vine. Also, living 'in a person' is an unclear concept to Rangi speakers—and even to me."

Realizing the team's struggle, the translation consultant asked questions to guide their search for a better expression. Finally, they found a figure of speech that the Rangi use to describe two very good friends, or a couple who love one another very much. The expression in Rangi literally means "to be one thing."

"When we put this expression in our translation," recalled Paulo, "I pictured my grandfather sitting with his best friend. My eyes were teary because that helped me visualize my relationship with Jesus. When I live in him, I am one thing with him. I saw how Jesus takes care of me. I could feel his love, and I could see a whole new life with him."

The Rangi team's consultant encouraged them to test it in the community. "We asked people what this means," said Paulo, "to abide in Jesus. Right away, they gave examples of people who are very close friends."

I love hearing stories like this—stories of individuals and even whole communities whose lives are changed when they truly understand God's Word in a way that makes sense. This need to abide in Jesus is crucial to our relationship with him; we need to be one with him in order to grow, thrive, and succeed. And that's done through intentional time with his Word as we water the soil of our hearts and souls.

I'm grateful that I can work toward consistently nurturing the spiritual soul of my relationship with Jesus, even if I have a hard time gauging the amount of water that my plants may or may not need! May we all seek "to be one thing" with Jesus each and every day.

SOWING SEEDS

The Rangi people have portions of Scripture available to them in their own language, but translation is still ongoing. Pray that more Scripture would be made available in Rangi so that they can continue to experience his love and the promise of being “one thing” with God.

Mimi ni mzabibu, ninyi ni matawi. Akaaye ndani yangu, nami ndani yake, huyo huzaa sana, maana pasipo mimi ninyi hamwezi kufanya jambo lolote.

Yohana 15:5

John 15:5 from the Kiswahili Contemporary Version by Biblica, a Wycliffe partner organization

DAY 10

A HARVEST OF BLESSING

So let's not get tired of doing what is good.
At just the right time we will reap a harvest of
blessing if we don't give up. —Galatians 6:9

Prayer has always been an important part of our family's foundation. From the time our kids were young, I (Kelly) would pray Scripture over them like Paul's words in the epistles or David's words in the psalms.

It was my hope and desire that we'd teach our kids the importance of prayer at a young age, and that they'd realize that their prayers mattered to God too! That's why I love the story of Sam Anderson so much.

At just five years old, Sam decided to pray for the people of Easter Island to receive God's Word. His parents, John and Joy Anderson, were missionaries with Wycliffe Bible Translators.

Sam would receive an allowance and tithe part of it toward supporting a Wycliffe translation project somewhere in the world. A large map was near the donation box where people could place a pin indicating a location and people group they wanted to pray for and support.

Sam studied the map and was interested in Easter Island, located more than two thousand miles off the west coast of Chile in the Pacific Ocean. But there was one problem with Sam's choice: A translation project on the island hadn't been started yet. So Sam told his parents that he would pray for one to start.

As Sam began to pray for Easter Island, he was unaware of how God was working in the lives of Bob and Nancy Weber, who had grown up in Peru and, like Sam, were children of Wycliffe missionaries. The Webers had married around the time Sam began to first pray for Easter Island and were asking God how he wanted to use them to further Bible translation.

Months later, Sam's parents received a letter from a friend in SIL* who mentioned that Bob and Nancy were being assigned to a new project on Easter Island! The Webers needed to first focus on helping the Rapa Nui people strengthen their language—which was facing possible extinction—and then to work with them to translate the New Testament.

The Webers discovered that Sam had begun praying for someone to start a translation for the people of Easter Island. They told him when they had first been interested in Easter Island—just after he started praying in 1975!

Now, more than forty-five years later, the Rapa Nui have the complete New Testament and portions of Scripture!

It gives me chills to think about the years of faithfulness displayed in Sam and the Weber's story—and ultimately that of the Rapa Nui people! The fact that Sam's prayers not only made a difference but that he learned about the harvest that had been reaped is an incredible testament of God's power and his hand at work around the world. What an honor and a privilege for Sam and his family to be a part of the Rapa Nui's journey. And to think that it all started when Sam was just five years old!

**Wycliffe's primary strategic partner.*

SOWING SEEDS

What legacy of faith can you leave by beginning a prayer journey with Jesus today? Is there something that you can pray for faithfully day after day, year after year, trusting that God will answer in his perfect timing?

DAY 11

LOVE GOD WITH ALL YOUR STRENGTH

Listen, O Israel! The Lord is our God, the Lord alone. And you must love the Lord your God with all your heart, all your soul, and all your strength. And you must commit yourselves wholeheartedly to these commands that I am giving you today. —Deuteronomy 6:4-6

"Give it all you've got!"

"Leave it all on the field."

Have you heard these phrases before? Have you used them? I (John) have. In fact, a high work ethic is something that has been instilled in me since childhood. But I realize I've incorrectly applied this works-centric line of thinking into my relationship with my heavenly Father.

If you do a web search for quotes about strength, you'll find more than 360 million hits. If you simply browse the word "strength," you'll get over one billion hits. We long to be strong, whether that means brute physical strength or mental and inner strength.

There are fifty-two different words throughout Scripture, in both Greek and Hebrew, that can be translated as "strength." Some of those words refer to physical might, but others refer to spiritual strength—strength of heart, mind, and soul. And still others refer to power or dominion.

But in Deuteronomy 6:4-6, the word translated as "strength" doesn't refer to the kind of strength we usually think of.

Here, it's the Hebrew word *me'od*, meaning "exceedingly, vehemently, forcefully, utterly, abundantly, wholly, with 'muchness' (as in greatness in quantity, measurement, or degree)." When Jesus calls us to love God with all our heart, soul, mind, and strength, he's calling us to love God with our everything.

Loving God with all our me'od means loving him with everything that we are, everything that we do and say, and everything that we have been given. Every moment, opportunity, ability, and capacity God gives us is to be used to love and honor him. To love God with all our me'od is to love him without limit. It's a call to love God with all of our "muchness."

In loving God with all my "heart, soul, mind, and strength" I have, at times, chosen to live out strength as doing more for the Lord. "Giving it all I've got" to ministry. "Leaving it all on the field" and wearing myself out by doing more.

This isn't what Jesus meant when he talked about loving God with all our strength. "Strength," when used in this context, means giving with "all of our being" and "our whole self." It doesn't mean doing more things. In fact, we can diminish our ability to fully engage with "all of our strength" if our sole focus is on doing.

I cannot give my best to knowing God when I am worn out from doing things for God. When I'm focused on doing things at the expense of my relationship with him, I end up relying on my own strength instead of existing from the outpouring of his strength. When left unchecked, relying on my own strength instead of God's leads to exhaustion, feeling overworked, and even experiencing burnout.

But in Christian ministry, we sometimes quietly applaud people who are "busy"; they must be loving God with all their strength, right? After all, they're doing so much for the Kingdom!

It's easy to equate working for God with loving him with all our strength. But I want my service to flow out of my relationship with God and love for him. I want to be a person who pursues a relationship with my heavenly Father with all my strength of being and with fervent energy and passion.

SOWING SEEDS

How can you step back and take a look at your life, assessing the motivation and reason behind the ways you tangibly choose to love God? What might it look like to intentionally choose to love him with all your strength—all of your "muchness"—without feeling like you have a long to-do list to showcase your love?

DAY 12

LOVE CHANGES EVERYTHING

But God showed his great love for us by sending Christ to die for us while we were still sinners.
— Romans 5:8

Over the years, I've (Kelly) shared the truth of God's unconditional love with others, and I've seen lives changed as a result of his lavish love and grace. While I shared that truth so readily with others, I didn't always live it out personally.

For years I let the enemy convince me that I had to earn God's love. While I knew I was a "new creation" in Christ, every time I messed up, I felt insecure in God's love for me. I allowed my identity to be rooted in my performance (or lack thereof), not in the grace and unconditional love of God. It wasn't until my mid-twenties that I realized I had the wrong perspective of that love.

I had followed Jesus for so long. How could I have misunderstood his love and grace toward me personally? How did I miss the invitation to simply receive his love? Why did I add conditions to it?

One thing I do know is that I'm so grateful God opened my eyes!

Living loved is our response to being known by God. While it's impossible to fully comprehend God's extravagant love for us, we're given a glimpse of one person who "lived loved" in Luke 7:36-50 when we read the story of the woman who poured perfume on Jesus's feet and wiped it with her hair.

Jesus knew who was anointing his feet. He knew her sin and offered forgiveness. The woman responded in worship and humble gratitude because she experienced God's love. As she anointed Jesus's feet with perfume, she expressed what it means to live loved. She was no longer defined by her past; Christ set her free to live loved through his grace and forgiveness.

Living loved isn't just our response to being known by God; it's our response to being changed by him. We are new creations! Our sins are forgiven! "The old life is gone; a new life has begun!" (2 Cor. 5:17b)

God invites us to receive his love. When we stop striving and simply receive, his Spirit changes us from the inside out.

To live loved also means to abide in Christ's extravagant love. Abiding in this way means that we let his love establish itself permanently within our souls and continually exert its power over us. Since Christ's love is rooted in his mercy, grace, and truth, it sets us free to be who God created us to be. And it changes everything!

SOWING SEEDS

How do you view yourself in light of your identity in Christ? Do you try to measure up to a certain standard, or are you able to live in grace and the knowledge that you are loved, in spite of all your shortcomings?

DAY 13

THE RIGHT PATH

Direct your children onto the right path,
and when they are older, they will not leave it.
—Proverbs 22:6

We have seven kids. As you can imagine, our house was often a loud and busy place!

Our kids were all different: different personalities, preferences, interests; there were introverts and extroverts, athletes and musicians. We had to find ways to meet each kid where they were at and help them through life's various ups and downs. The one thing that was constant was our desire to raise our kids according to Scripture. We wanted them to know God's love and in turn to raise them to love Jesus and serve him with their whole heart and with all of their life—whatever that looks like.

Our heavenly Father views us the same way. We're all different: We have different backgrounds, cultures, languages, and family dynamics. But he wants all of us to know that he loves us—and he wants that understanding to happen in a way that we can clearly understand.

As parents, this story about a Romanian pastor hits a special spot in our hearts.

> The Romanian pastor wasn't sure what to do. He had adopted a Deaf boy into his family and wanted to teach him about the Bible. But after trying for a while, the hearing pastor could

> tell that his Deaf son didn't understand the Scripture in spoken and written Romanian.
>
> Then one day, the pastor saw a video depicting a New Testament passage. The story was of Jesus calming the storm—and it was in Romanian Sign Language (RSL). When the father showed the video to his son, the boy perked up and seemed to clearly understand the story's message.
>
> Excitedly, the pastor reached out to the Romanian Sign Language translation team who created the video. The team members soon connected the family to a local Deaf church, where the boy was able to form relationships with other Deaf believers while growing in his faith through Scripture—communicated in a language and format that impacts his heart.

There are more than ninety thousand Deaf people living across Romania who use Romanian Sign Language to communicate. Culturally, they view themselves as members of a vibrant community with its own unique language and identity—a language and identity that is known and loved by our wonderful Father God.

Some Deaf people have been members of Christian churches in Romania for many years, but due to communication challenges with society around them and limited access to God's Word, they haven't been able to be discipled.

As translators continue to work on the Romanian Sign Language Bible translation, praise God that stories of hope and transformation are already emerging as people engage with available Scripture portions.

It's the same with us, isn't it? When we try to engage with someone in a way that doesn't connect with them, we're only able to get so far. Maybe we're able to achieve a surface, artificial level of understanding. But it isn't until we communicate with them in a way they clearly understand—which for this little boy was Romanian Sign Language—that lives are transformed. Praise God that this little boy is now being raised with Scripture in his language so that his life can be set on the right path!

SOWING SEEDS

There are more than 350 sign languages around the world, and only one—American Sign Language—has the complete Bible.*

Pray for these communities to receive God's Word in a language and format they can clearly understand! For a glimpse of different sign language projects in progress, visit Wycliffe's partner organization Deaf Bible, at **deaf.bible** today.

**This is based on the translation standards established by the Forum of Bible Agencies International. The American Sign Language Bible was completed by Deaf Missions in collaboration with partners like American Bible Society, Seed Company, DOOR International, Deaf Bible Society, Pioneer Bible Translators, and Wycliffe Bible Translators USA.*

RSL team signing "Jesus loves you."

DAY 14

LOVE GOD WITH ALL YOUR MIND

Those who are dominated by the sinful nature think about sinful things, but those who are controlled by the Holy Spirit think about things that please the Spirit. So letting your sinful nature control your mind leads to death. But letting the Spirit control your mind leads to life and peace.
—Romans 8:5-6

When our kids were young, we often went camping in the mountains of Colorado. The beauty of God's creation was captivating—the sounds of a bubbling stream, birds singing, elk bugling in the fall. I (Kelly) loved setting up camp in that temporary home.

God has used the image of setting up camp to remind me of more than just his incredible creation; he's used it as a metaphor for my thought life.

When someone has offended or injured us with their words, do we allow hurt to "set up camp" in our minds, affecting our perspectives and interactions with that person? Or do we let the truth of God's Word take up residence instead to bring life and grace to our thoughts?

While we can't control the thoughts that enter our heads, we can control what we do with those thoughts. And we need to be proactive in dealing with wrong thinking. We must learn to recognize and deal with thoughts that aren't in line with the truth of God's Word. As we acknowledge wrongful thinking, we should take each thought captive and make it obedient to Christ. In other words, we don't allow our minds to dwell on wrong thoughts—we evict them. We then replace those thoughts with God's perspective, truth, and love.

That's why I think the call to love God with all our minds is one of the hardest parts of maturing as believers. The Bible has a lot to say about our minds—from how to deal with sin that begins as a seed there, to exhortation on what to think about, to how to take our thoughts captive and realign them with the truth of God's Word.

Jesus calls us to love God with all our minds. The Greek word for "mind" in Mark 12:30 is *dianoia*, and it refers to the mind as a faculty of understanding, feeling, and desiring. It covers everything from our deepest thoughts to our imaginations, both good or bad.

We fill our minds by remembering and meditating on the truth and love of God. We need to remember who God is and what he's done and consistently meditate on those truths.

But remembering is more than just bringing something to our minds. It's also defined this way: "to keep in mind; to remain aware of." To meditate is "to attend to, practice; be diligent in; ponder, imagine."

So how can we be intentional with thoughts that just seem to pop into our heads?

We must first recognize thoughts that aren't in line with the truth of God's Word. As we acknowledge wrong thinking, we need to take each thought captive and make it obedient to Christ. In other words, we evict the wrong thoughts. We kick them out of our camp. But loving God with all our minds is more than just removing wrong thoughts; we need to replace them with God's perspective, truth and love.

When we align our thoughts with the truth of God's Word, our perspective of our circumstances and of others changes. But most importantly, realigning our thoughts reflects our love for God.

SOWING SEEDS

What are you allowing into your mind today? Take some time to assess your thoughts and the channels of influence you have in your day-to-day rhythms. How can you seek to proactively choose what you allow into your mind?

DAY 15

THINK-STEW

And now, dear brothers and sisters, one final thing. Fix your thoughts on what is true, and honorable, and right, and pure, and lovely, and admirable. Think about things that are excellent and worthy of praise.
—Philippians 4:8

Do you ever have a thought that just continues to roll around in your head? Or perhaps you have a mental to-do list and until that last item is checked off, you're incapable of moving on and letting it go?

If you're like us, you've had at least one time in your life when you've felt anxious, worried, or with the nagging sense that you need to get something done before you can truly rest. You wake up, and that one thing is on your mind; you go to bed, and it's the last thing you think about. It can be difficult to let go. We're captive to the thought, the agenda, the worry, or fear that we're carrying with us.

John Nystrom is a Wycliffe translation consultant. He shared the following story from the Arop language project in Papua New Guinea that he's serving with:

> I was helping Emil Ninkure, a translator for the Arop language in Papua New Guinea, with his translation of Philippians 3 and 4. In verses six and eight, he used an Arop word, *aknieyjawana*. In the Arop draft Paul tells the Philippians not to think-stew about anything, but to hand their "heavies" over to God as

> they pray. But in verse eight Paul tells them they should think-stew (aknieyjawana) about whatever is noble, whatever is right, pure, lovely, admirable, excellent, or praiseworthy. So what does aknieyjawana mean—to be anxious or to meditate in a positive way? Neither one and both. It means to continually and thoroughly think about something all the way through. Whether that produces anxiety or peace depends on what we're thinking-stewing about.

Think-stew is a great way to describe what Paul is talking about in Philippians 4 when he tells us to fix our thoughts on "what is true, and honorable, and right, and pure, and lovely, and admirable" (v. 8a). When you make a stew, you know that the longer it cooks, the richer the flavor; the better the end product. The same is true for our own lives—but we need to be intentional and careful about what we're thinking-stewing about!

So what about you? What are you going to fix your thoughts on? How are you going to intentionally surrender whatever is laying heavy on your heart and mind and instead think about what is true, honorable, right, pure, lovely, admirable, excellent, and worthy of praise?

SOWING SEEDS

Write out Philippians 4:8 and place it somewhere you'll see it every day—on your bathroom mirror to read as you brush your teeth or on the wall above your stove as you cook. Memorize these words and think of ways that you can fix your thoughts on what is true, honorable, right, pure, lovely, admirable, excellent, and worthy of praise.

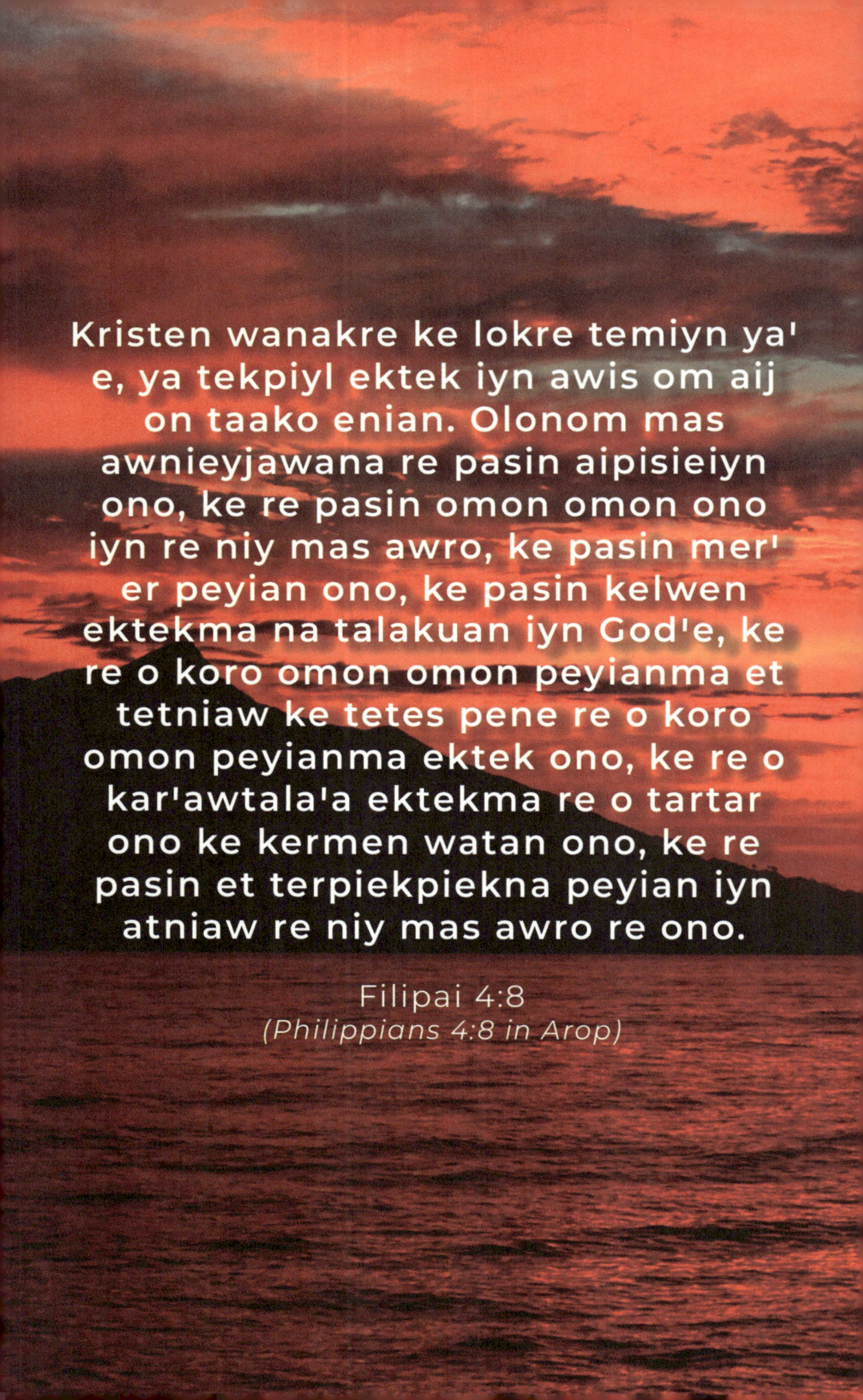

Kristen wanakre ke lokre temiyn ya'
e, ya tekpiyl ektek iyn awis om aij
on taako enian. Olonom mas
awnieyjawana re pasin aipisieiyn
ono, ke re pasin omon omon ono
iyn re niy mas awro, ke pasin mer'
er peyian ono, ke pasin kelwen
ektekma na talakuan iyn God'e, ke
re o koro omon omon peyianma et
tetniaw ke tetes pene re o koro
omon peyianma ektek ono, ke re o
kar'awtala'a ektekma re o tartar
ono ke kermen watan ono, ke re
pasin et terpiekpiekna peyian iyn
atniaw re niy mas awro re ono.

Filipai 4:8

(Philippians 4:8 in Arop)

You all must think-stew about true things, and things that are good-good that people should do, and things that are straight, and things that are clean in the eye of God, and the things that are totally good-good that we see and say that they are really good, and the things that totally surpass everything else and are first-rate, and the things that we totally rejoice to see and people should do.

Philippians 4:8

(translated from Arop back into English)

DAY 16

STOP AND SMELL THE ROSES

For as the earth bursts with spring wildflowers, and as a garden cascades with blossoms, so the Master, God, brings righteousness into full bloom and puts praise on display before the nations.
—Isaiah 61:11 (MSG)

There's nothing quite like seeing things through the eyes of a child.

Some evenings John and I take a walk with our grandchildren to a nearby pond. Along the way we encounter plenty of opportunities for exploration. A few years ago, our then three-year-old grandson, Aidan, would declare: "Look, Nana! An ant! An' anudder ant! Nana! Here's anudder one!" You can't imagine how many ants he "discovers" in this short walk.

But each encounter creates delight for our grandson. As we watch his awe and wonder over such seemingly insignificant creatures, we too experience a new sense of awe and wonder at God's creativity. Aidan also has a tender heart toward God's creativity displayed through flowers—everything from a tiny weed to a full flower bush catches his attention, and he sweetly insists on stopping and picking them to create a bouquet for me. Once we get home from our walk, he'll quickly dash to his "kids cupboard" to pull out a plastic cup, fill it with water, and lovingly arrange the flowers before delivering the bouquet to me. You can tell he absolutely delights not only in these beautiful flowers, but in cultivating and arranging their beauty as a gift to me.

It reminds me of a story shared from the Rangi translation team in Tanzania. One day they were working on translating the phrase "Garden of Eden" in Genesis 13:10. The Swahili word the translators used was *bustani*. But this word didn't conjure up anything special or beautiful about a garden; it simply meant "garden."

The translation consultant working with the team described how beautiful the Garden of Eden must have been—a wondrous place filled with water, animals, trees, flowers, and more.

During the discussion, two of the Rangi translators, Paulo and Maingu, "saw" that visual in their mind for the first time. They realized that the best Rangi word for a beautiful garden was actually *ntindika*, not bustani. Paulo described ntindika as a place which, even though people need to tend and cultivate it, never fails to produce a great variety of delicious fruit. Paulo said, "You can always find food there."

That's when the team agreed—they had found the right word for the Garden of Eden.

When translators work, it's crucial that they choose the correct word to convey an accurate, authentic meaning of the Scripture to the community. They have to cultivate and arrange the words just right, so that the full lavish beauty of God's Word is revealed.

Just like Aidan revels in the beauty of God's creation, so we too are given the chance to revel in his Word when we can clearly understand it. And when that happens, God's praise and might are displayed in perfect majesty.

SOWING SEEDS

Translation work is ongoing for the Rangi community and many communities like them. As Scripture is made accessible, they're given the chance to experience God's goodness in a language and format they can clearly understand. What a glorious day it will be when all languages are able to understand God's Word for themselves, just as they are able to experience the beauty of creation that declares his praises!

DAY 17

THE LOVE OF GOD IN SIGN LANGUAGE

"And this gospel of the kingdom will be proclaimed throughout the whole world as a testimony to all nations . . ." —Matthew 24:14a (ESV)

Wycliffe's vision is for people from every language to understand the Bible and be transformed. Our mission is to serve with the global body of Christ to advance Bible translation and work together so people can encounter God through his Word. And that's exactly what is happening for communities around the world today, including the Japanese Deaf.

The Deaf are considered to be the largest unreached people group. And because they're a minority, the Deaf are often at a disadvantage when it comes to operating within a hearing culture.

When Uiko Yani first started working on the Japanese Sign Language (JSL) translation project, she wasn't a Christian. When she did encounter Christians, Uiko was told she needed to read the Japanese Bible to understand God. But because she's Deaf, she wasn't interested in learning more about Christianity.

On and off until 2009, however, Uiko worked with ViBi* because she needed a job and enjoyed translation. She became a full-time staff member in 2009, and her first job was to work on the book of Matthew.

**Short for VisualBible*

"Eventually I started translating the book of Matthew, and I started wondering, 'Is this the Word of God?' It was totally different from what I was told as a child. I was told that it was all about rules and obeying the rules," Uiko signed. "Instead, it was all about what love is and what God has done for us. So I thought to myself, 'Maybe what I've thought was true about God was actually wrong.' I got to know God through translating the Bible. And that's how I got to understand why God is who he is, and became [a] Christian."

Today Uiko is passionate about Scripture and its holistic impact on the Deaf in Japan. The Deaf community in the country is small to begin with, and the Christian population among the Deaf is even smaller. Her desire is that the JSL Bible will transform people's hearts and the way that they see their value in God's eyes.

People like Uiko make the work of Bible translation so meaningful. When we see people transformed after encountering God in both a language and format they clearly understand, we can't help but walk away changed! As Uiko and the JSL team continue to translate the Bible, they are starting a chain of events which will impact generations to come.

Every sign matters. And every sign points to Jesus and to his amazing, transformational love.

SOWING SEEDS

God is doing amazing things in sign language communities around the world! Join us in praying for Deaf communities to receive Scripture in a language and format they clearly understand. What a glorious day that will be!

DAY 18

THE WAY, THE TRUTH, AND THE LIFE

Jesus told him, "I am the way, the truth, and the life. No one can come to the Father except through me."
—John 14:6

John and I grew up in Christian homes. John's dad was in the Air Force, and my parents served as medical missionaries in the Philippines. There's never been a time where our families weren't involved in church, or a time that we can remember what life was like before Jesus. Not everyone is as blessed as we are to have a heritage of faith and relationship with the Lord.

Nur lived in a community in southwestern Ethiopia where Christians were often not accepted. They were persecuted, and their houses were even burned to the ground. But God had called Nur to help finish the job of translating the New Testament for the Seze people. Despite opposition, the Spirit was at work preparing even the hardest of hearts to receive God's Word.

One of those hearts belonged to Ali, a man who seemed to despise the gospel. He was well known for tormenting Christians in the community. No one dared to speak to him about Jesus. Then one night that all began to change.

Ali dreamed of a man dressed in white who said, "I am the way, the truth, and the life." It was a dream Ali tried to forget because he knew the man was Jesus. But he couldn't ignore it any longer.

So Ali began secretly attending a church in another community to learn more about Jesus. There, a courageous believer took him under his wing and explained the Scriptures to him. Ali chose to follow Christ.

As a result, Ali and his family were attacked by their neighbors and driven from their community. But Ali felt God's call to share the Good News of Jesus and led thirty people to Christ. After that, Ali joined Nur on the Seze translation team.

"I can't wait until I can hold the full Seze Bible in my hands as I talk to my community about Jesus," Ali said.

Tragically, both Nur and Ali were killed by those who oppose Christianity in early 2021. But the translation team is not stopping their work until the job is finished. They've seen how God is using his Word to proclaim the hope of the gospel and bring others to faith in Jesus—just like Ali.

When Saul of Tarsus met Jesus on the road to Emmaus, he was transformed from a persecutor of Christians to a martyr for the name of Christ, and that power is still at work in Ethiopia. God is on the move as translation work continues to happen, both in Ethiopia and around the world.

Jesus told us that he is the way, the truth, and the life. He never promised that the road before us would be easy, but he's always with us. Oh, that we would all be transformed—just like Saul, Nur, and Ali—as we encounter Jesus.

SOWING SEEDS

Around the world there are stories of people just like Nur and Ali who are laying down their lives for their faith. Pray that God would equip and empower them to be strong in the faith, and ask God to reveal how you can also stand strong in your own faith

DAY 19

THE BREAD OF LIFE

Jesus replied, "I am the bread of life.
Whoever comes to me will never be hungry again.
Whoever believes in me will never be thirsty."
—John 6:35

Have you ever had a day where it just feels like no matter what or how much you eat, you're never fully satisfied? Maybe it's that you keep snacking, grabbing quick and easy food that only temporarily fills you up but doesn't truly nourish you. Or maybe you have a food that you eat if you're feeling stressed (chocolate and peanut butter candies are a must in our household!) that might make you feel good in the moment but doesn't satisfy you for long.

If we're completely honest with ourselves, we've all used distractions like TV, online shopping, or even busyness itself to try and fill us up. In the Western context, we've often been trained—whether explicitly or implicitly—to seek comfort in anything that we think of to get a quick fix. But there's a source of eternal satisfaction that we should be turning to instead: God's Word.

In John 6:32-35, we see Jesus talking to a crowd of people. They want him to show them a miraculous sign, like when God gave the Israelites manna in the desert, so that they'll believe in him.

> Jesus said, "I tell you the truth, Moses didn't give you bread from heaven. My Father did. And now he offers you the true bread from

> heaven. The true bread of God is the one who comes down from heaven and gives life to the world."
>
> "Sir," they said, "give us that bread every day."
>
> Jesus replied, "I am the bread of life. Whoever comes to me will never be hungry again. Whoever believes in me will never be thirsty."

We have access to Jesus through the Bible. Inside the pages of Scripture, we see the full scope of God's story, of his great love, and of his purpose and plan for our lives. Each day we should be studying it, devouring it, and filling ourselves up with him. It is a privilege and a blessing that we often take for granted, choosing instead to "snack" on Scripture when we need God's comfort, hope, and peace, rather than treating it like the feast that it truly is.

John Atsu Sagbavu is a Siwu translator in Ghana. When he was asked why it's important for the Siwu people to have both the New and Old Testaments translated, he responded: "Having the New Testament without the Old Testament is just like having your raw bread without tea or oats. So you'll be half-fed. To be fully fed and satisfied, we need the Old Testament."

And that is Wycliffe's hope and prayer: that one day all people would have access to the full counsel of God's Word in a language and format they clearly understand. We don't want them to only be able to snack on Scripture; we want them to have this lavish, rich feast for themselves. What an honor and privilege it is for us to be able to partner in this work so that more and more people can meet Jesus, the bread of life.

SOWING SEEDS

Next time you reach for a snack to satisfy your physical hunger, what if you paired it with reading a Scripture to feed you spiritually as well? How amazing it would be if we turned to Scripture for sustenance as frequently as we turn to food for physical nourishment!

Yesu ɔɣere ma sɔ, “Mme
nɖe ngbã aɖera wamɔ
ne. Ngɔ loba wũ kɔrɛ ne,
kukã iibakpɛ̃ wũ kunya,
fiɛ ngɔ lofɔ me ɔɖe ne,
ɔme iibakore wũ ɔnya.

Yohanes 6:35

(John 6:35 in Siwu)

DAY 20

THE LIGHT THAT LEADS TO LIFE

Jesus spoke to the people once more and said,
"I am the light of the world. If you follow me,
you won't have to walk in darkness, because you
will have the light that leads to life."
—John 8:12

In the Philippines, we'd often have power outages after a storm. Sometimes they'd last for a few hours, and other times they'd last for days. Filipinos called power outages "brownouts"—not "blackouts." To Filipinos, "blackouts" were when power was out for weeks at a time, like what had happened in many places across the country during World War II.

Whenever we'd have a brownout, our seven kids would often emerge from their bedrooms with blankets and pillows in tow to wait out the darkness together in our *sala*, or living room. There they could watch the storm through our slatted glass windows together, not having to fear the darkness around them. When dusk would come, we'd light a few candles to help dispel the shadows as we prepared for bed and waited for the power to turn back on.

These brownouts were physical and temporary. But for millions of people around the world, they're experiencing spiritual blackouts—and they may not even know it.

That's what makes stories like this one bring joy to our hearts:

Bennis, an audio technician for the *JESUS* film, noticed a change in the young Siarlak man's voice and pressed the "pause" button. Bennis had been watching the lines on the computer screen as the man read the voice of Jesus for the recording. The young man had tears in his eyes and got choked up as he explained to the recording team, "I can't read this Jesus part. My heart is not ready for this role. Jesus touches my life too much!"

For some participating in the recording, it was the first time they had ever read the Bible in their own language, and they were moved to tears at the beauty of the words.

When the *JESUS* film recording was finished, it was time for the Siarlak people to watch it in their language. As the movie began and the crowd saw men and women on the screen playing the parts from the Gospel of Luke, they asked each other: "When did these foreigners learn our language?" The recording team explained to them that some of their own people were speaking the words.

Men, women, and children sat on the ground and watched the film unfold. When they saw Jesus being nailed to the cross, the whole group fell silent. Bennis testified, "I could feel the emotion in the crowd, and I knew the Holy Spirit was working."

Afterward, some of the women said, "In our local language the message is so simple and we can understand the meaning much more clearly than before. It was like a light passed before us!"

Jesus is the light of the world, and as followers of Jesus it is our privilege and responsibility to shine his light wherever we go. Together we can help dispel the spiritual blackout for communities around the world as they are introduced to his light and love in their own language.

SOWING SEEDS

Wycliffe partners with The Jesus Film Project which takes the translated Gospel of Luke and dubs it to the *JESUS* film. They also produce other Jesus-centric videos. Today these videos are available in more than 1,800 languages and introduce people to a visual representation of Jesus's life in a language they clearly understand.

Visit **jesusfilm.org** to learn more and to get a glimpse of the *JESUS* film for yourself.

DAY 21

THE POWER OF PRAISE

For you are my hiding place; you protect me from trouble. You surround me with songs of victory.
—Psalm 32:7

Music has always been an important part of our lives. In fact, we met because of music! (Short version of that story is that Kelly was dared by a friend to try to make John break a smile by making silly faces at him while he sang. By the end of the concert, he wanted to meet her and the rest is history.)

During our years in the pastorate, we often sang duets for special occasions or friends' weddings. Now we're enjoying music with our grandkids and love hearing their little voices sing songs of praise to our God!

It's often easy to praise God through music. After all, music is a powerful, compelling way to elicit emotion. But what about the times when we don't feel like praising God?

Jan Benson is a retired Wycliffe translator, and she shared the following story with us:

> I'll never forget the blue skies and Andean landscapes that were such a fitting backdrop as our car rumbled along the dusty road back to town. The other missionaries and I were rejoicing at all we had seen God do while out among the Quechua villagers.

As we rounded a switchback road, we noticed a truck down below making its way up the narrow mountain road. We pulled over to let it pass, but it didn't. That's when we saw heavily armed men coming out of the truck to surround our vehicle. We knew instantly who they were: a Peruvian insurgent group. This group was widely known for violence that included public executions. All I could say was, "Jesus, help us!"

The men forced us into their vehicle. As I sat huddled in a corner of the truck's cabin, I was filled with terror. "What was happening? Where were they taking us? Would we be tortured or worse?" A fear gripped me like nothing I had ever experienced.

And then, seemingly out of nowhere, a thought came through loud and clear: "God inhabits the praise of his people!" But how could I praise God?

Words came, and I began to sing a worship song based on Psalm 32:7, which says: "For you are my hiding place; you protect me from trouble. You surround me with songs of victory."

I soon became aware that Jesus was sitting on the bench right beside me, going through this nightmare with me. A trickle of peace soon became a flood. His presence became more tangible to me than the lurching truck, my captors, their guns, and hate. I felt Jesus's all-encompassing love—so real, powerful, and personal.

> My fear was replaced by the joy of intimate communion with him. I knew that nothing could take that from me—not even death itself. I had never felt safer or closer to him than I did in that moment.

How can you choose to praise God in the good times and the bad, no matter what you might be facing? How can you, just like Jan, lead your heart to a posture of praise when your head might be screaming the opposite at you?

Praise is powerful. It can redirect our attitude, our thoughts, and our fears when we choose to praise God. We can't wait for the day when every nation, language, and people will praise God together in heaven!

SOWING SEEDS

Do you have a favorite worship song? Play it now and take a few minutes to praise God through music, asking that he would help the truth of those lyrics to reign true in your life regardless of your circumstances.

DAY 22

TRUST AND BELIEVE

". . . I know the one in whom I trust, and I am sure that he is able to guard what I have entrusted to him until the day of his return."
—2 Timothy 1:12b

Trust. It's not something we hand out haphazardly.

Many people don't extend trust to someone else without it being earned first. We learn to trust people who support what they say through their actions or evidence.

We serve a God whose actions support his words. We see this throughout Scripture; God is who he says he is, and he can do what he says he can do.

But what happens when God doesn't act the way we think he should or when things don't turn out the way we hoped? Is he any less trustworthy? Any less believable?

There's a big difference between believing God and believing in God. The Israelites believed in God; they saw his power at work in miraculous ways as he brought them out of Egypt. God did what he said he would do. Time and time again, he proved himself worthy of the Israelites' trust. Yet the moment circumstances became difficult or challenging, they lost sight of his trustworthiness and believability.

They believed in God, but they didn't believe him.

Believing God and trusting him go hand-in-hand. Trusting God doesn't come from head knowledge; it comes from a personal relationship with him.

Sai* is blind, but he doesn't let that deter him from walking with God. Sai committed his life to Jesus Christ a few years ago. One day there was a torrential downpour, but Sai grabbed his walking stick anyway and started an arduous uphill climb to reach a house church where he could hear the audio Scriptures in his language. Drenched and breathing heavily, Sai leaned against his stick and called out, "Brother, can you help me climb?"

The approaching Bible translation team immediately recognized Sai and quickly assisted him. The team was inspired by his commitment. "It was breathtaking to see a blind man [overcome his struggles to] hear the audio Bible," a staff member later said.

Since that encounter, the New Testament has been completed in Sai's language and he now plays the audio Scripture for his friends and neighbors. When they hear the stories of Jesus in their language, they're receptive to the truth of God's Word.

Sai's story is such an encouragement, isn't it? Sometimes we can be quick to let our circumstances—rather than God's proven character—shape what we believe about him. But when we stop and look at our circumstances through the lens of our relationship with God and his trustworthiness, we can respond in faith and belief. There's a certainty that he will indeed work all things for our good, making us more like Jesus in the process.

And that's exactly what Sai did. Even though he's blind and a storm was raging, he kept his focus on Jesus.

**Name changed.*

He continued to climb, continued to move forward, trusting God every step of the way.

Every opportunity that comes our way is a chance to trust God more. Through our relationship with Christ, we experience his love, grace, and mercy at work in our lives and in our circumstances.

The more we know him, the more we trust and believe him.

SOWING SEEDS

Intentional time in Scripture helps you build the foundation for trusting in God for all things. Read these Scriptures and be encouraged as you continue to grow in your relationship with him.

- Proverbs 3:5-6
- Psalm 37:4-5
- Isaiah 26:3
- Psalm 9:10
- Isaiah 12:2
- Psalm 56:3
- Jeremiah 17:7

SONIKA
Faith Comes
By Hearing

DAY 23

ACTIONS SPEAK LOUDER THAN WORDS

"Your love for one another will prove to the world that you are my disciples." —John 13:35

One of the primary ways I (Kelly) receive love—and how I often choose to give love to others—is through words of affirmation. Whether it's a word of encouragement or a sweet note from a loved one, I thrive on thoughtful words. They fill my "love tank" so that I can continue to pour out love to those around me as well.

Meanwhile, John's primary way to give and receive love is through acts of service. Over the years I've watched him serve in a variety of ways, whether something as simple as consistently mowing the lawn each week, helping a family member or friend move, or by taking the time to listen and give counsel to someone. Both of our love languages—words of affirmation and acts of service—are God-given gifts, but if we don't also practice loving each other in different ways, we might just miss the mark.

If I only love someone with words, they might feel encouraged in the moment. But what if my actions don't reinforce those words?

Or if I'm only serving someone externally but have a bad attitude about it internally, am I really showing love? I might appear to be "serving," but on the inside I might be grumbling the whole time.

Words and actions, when paired together, are a powerful way of loving others well. There's truth in the cliché: "Actions speak louder than words."

It's the same in our relationship with God. I can say that I love God. I can say that I love people. But do my actions reinforce those words? Am I living in such a way that my actions declare my love for God without a single word needing to be said?

John 13:35 says, "Your love for one another will prove to the world that you are my disciples."

Let's read that again: "*Your love for one another* will prove to the world that you are my disciples" (emphasis mine).

The action of loving is what gives truth and validity to the words we say. As we align our actions with our words in loving others we become the hands and feet of Jesus. This is our biblical call: "Let's not merely say that we love each other; let us show the truth by our actions" (1 John 3:18).

How are you living out the call?

SOWING SEEDS

Challenge yourself: commit to loving people with specific actions—a surprise gift, an unexpected act of service—without using words and see how others respond to your act of love.

DAY 24

PUT YOUR EARS ON

So faith comes from hearing, that is, hearing the Good News about Christ.
—Romans 10:17

Our family likes to holler. Growing up with seven kids in the home, you can imagine the hustle and bustle of our household. When trying to rally the troops, it was often easier to just holler things like, "Time for dinner!" or "Time for chores!" than it was to go from door to door and round them up.

There are definitely certain phrases that catch attention faster than others, right? There was more often than not a much more timely reaction to "Time for dinner!" than "Time for chores!" Our response is often tied to the heart of the message being relayed. We're much more likely to respond to something when it's good news (like announcing it's time to eat) versus when it's news that we don't want to hear (like telling your kids they need to clean up).

The same is true when sharing God's Word with people around the world. When the message is good for them to hear—when it's in a language and format they can clearly understand—it takes root in their hearts and stirs up action. But when the message is confusing or incoherent—such as when it's in a secondary language or one they don't understand as well—the response might be small, if there's any response at all.

The Yamap translation team in Papua New Guinea has experienced this as they share the Scriptures. They travel to different villages and settlements and call their trips “Yamap Patrols.” On these trips they stay in each area for a few days to teach the people to read the Yamap Scriptures and distribute booklets that include the Gospels of Matthew, Mark, Luke, and John. And the response to Scriptures in Yamap versus the national language of Tok Pisin is exactly why we believe that everyone needs the Bible in their own language!

“What I’ve seen on our patrols is that kids sit still and ‘put their ears’ [on] to hear when someone is reading the Yamap language,” said Isaac, one of the translators. “In church, when they hear Tok Pisin spoken and read, they move around and come and go like butterflies—they don’t sit still. When they hear Yamap, they don’t make a noise and they sit still and listen. The kids grow up with the language and they know it.”

Isaac continued: “The adults say that, ‘Yes, God’s Word came in Tok Pisin and we read it and know what it says; but when we read in Yamap, the "hidden talk" becomes clear and we understand.’”

We need to “put our ears on” to listen to Jesus’s words in order to understand and be transformed. Like Paul describes in Romans 10:17: “So faith comes from hearing, that is, hearing the Good News about Christ” (ESV). We are changed when we encounter the gospel. We experience faith when we “put our ears on” and receive God’s Word in a language and format that we clearly understand.

SOWING SEEDS

Communities around the world are able to "put their ears on" when they get access to God's Word. It's so important to understand Scripture for yourself in order to truly be transformed by God's grace! Pray for the millions of people around the world who are getting access to Scripture for the first time, and ask God to help them "put their ears on" so that they might be transformed forever.

DAY 25

THE GOOD SOIL

And the seeds that fell on the good soil represent honest, good-hearted people who hear God's word, cling to it, and patiently produce a huge harvest.
—Luke 8:15

You've likely heard the parable of the farmer scattering the seed (and if you haven't, stop and read Luke 8:4-15 for all the details). Some seed falls on a footpath, others on rocky soil. Some seed falls among thorns, which don't last or thrive.

But there is also seed that falls on good soil—soil that is fertile and ready to produce a great harvest.

We're the soil that Jesus is describing; our souls are waiting to be cultivated, ready to receive the seed that is God's Word. This seed is just waiting to blossom, to bloom, and to grow into a great harvest if only we care for our soil well.

But are we working to care for the soil of our souls? Are we watering and caring for it, or are we allowing our hearts to be hardened or distracted by what the world has to offer?

One of the privileges of working in an international missions-based organization is that we get to rejoice with communities around the world who are receiving the seeds of the gospel—often for the very first time! We have the privilege of hearing stories that encourage our hearts and remind us of why we do what we do. Simon's story is one such reminder:

Simon's muscles ached from the three-hour trek. Several months prior, he had attended a training workshop where he learned to craft oral Bible stories in his language, Oshie.

Now he wanted to share those stories in a nearby community. Transportation wasn't available due to civil unrest and the COVID-19 pandemic, so Simon decided to make the long journey on foot. Once he arrived, he went from house to house, inviting everyone to meet him at a local church.

"The people gathered and I told them two Bible stories," Simon said later. "The love of God touched their hearts so much that they pleaded with me to stay overnight and share stories with them again the next day."

He agreed to their request, and after the second storytelling time, many people couldn't stop talking about what they had experienced. "We have never heard God's Word in this way—in [our language]!" they said.

When it was finally time for Simon to leave, the community members asked him to visit again, and often. "This brought joy to my heart, seeing what God could do through the stories," he said. "I knew I wasn't just a storyteller. God has called me into the ministry to change lives through the oral Bible storytelling strategy."

Can you feel the people's hunger and thirst for more of God's Word as you read Simon's story? They are eagerly waiting to be spiritually fed from Scripture in their own language!

We are privileged to have access to God's Word whenever we want. But are we still striving to care for the soil of our hearts? Are we still watering and caring for the seeds, or are we allowing ourselves to grow hard, distracted by things that are not from God?

May our hearts be rich, fertile soil that grows a bountiful harvest so that we too can then be laborers in God's fields, sowing the seeds of the gospel for his glory and our ultimate good!

SOWING SEEDS

Oral communities around the world are learning about Jesus through stories shared verbally in their own language. Faith Comes By Hearing is a Wycliffe partner organization that is committed to helping millions of people with a preference for oral learning to hear about Jesus through audio Bible resources. Learn more about the importance of oral Bible translation at **faithcomesbyhearing.com**.

DAY 26

A SHINING LIGHT

We now have this light shining in our hearts, but we ourselves are like fragile clay jars containing this great treasure. This makes it clear that our great power is from God, not from ourselves. We are pressed on every side by troubles, but we are not crushed . . . We get knocked down, but we are not destroyed. Through suffering, our bodies continue to share in the death of Jesus so that the life of Jesus may also be seen in our bodies.
— 2 Corinthians 4:7-8a, 4:9b-10

You've likely heard of the phrase "first world problems." It's how many Western nations term the trivial inconveniences that we face that can put a damper on our day. Search the phrase online and you'll find a myriad of results, ranging in silliness.

We laugh at these "problems," but if we're honest with ourselves we all have first world problems! That's why it becomes even more humbling when we hear stories of people who have faced insurmountable hardships and difficulties, and still overcame—people like the Keliko of South Sudan.

The Keliko people lost everything—possessions, homes, and even their country. But hardships and trials were no match for them, because they've found the secret of joy in difficult times: hope and faith built upon God's Word.

In 1985, the Keliko didn't have the Bible in their language. In fact, their language hadn't even been written down! Pastor David Gale, a local Keliko pastor, went to a conference where he was asked to read or sing Scripture in his own language, but he couldn't participate because the Bible wasn't in Keliko. That's when a vision was sparked to see God's Word translated into Keliko.

A translation program was started, but civil unrest created many difficulties for the team and their families. As a result, the translation came to a halt before they could finish developing the written language.

The team continued to faithfully ask, seek, and knock—for ten long years. When God finally opened the door again, the team eagerly restarted their work. Despite having to move the translation to different locations and be away from their families, the translators wouldn't give up. Even when the Keliko were forced out of South Sudan in 2016 and scattered to refugee settlements in the Democratic Republic of the Congo and Uganda, the translation moved forward with a team of translators led by Pastor David's grandson.

The team persevered because they had a vision for the Keliko people to have God's Word in their language. On August 11, 2018, thirty-three years after Pastor David's vision came to life, the Keliko New Testament with Old Testament portions was dedicated in Uganda by his grandson and fellow translators.

Today the Keliko are still displaced and facing hardships, but you wouldn't know it from the joy expressed by the church. They received what they asked God for—Scripture in their own language!

In the days leading up to the dedication of their New Testament, the Keliko people joyfully sang the words of

Psalm 66:5 with a sense of victory: “Come and see what the Lord has done.”

The Keliko people have light shining in their hearts, just like Paul describes in 2 Corinthians 4. And even though they went through numerous trials and challenges, they still persevered. And because of that, future generations will be raised with God’s Word in their language! May we be encouraged and inspired by stories like the Keliko, and may we too be willing to do whatever it takes to spread Christ’s light and love to the world around us.

SOWING SEEDS

The Bible in Keliko is translated into English as “The Book of Joy.” This truth is so evident in this community as they have experienced joy even in the midst of insurmountable hardship and difficulty. Reflect on the ways God's Word has brought you joy, both in good times and in hard.

Ngá múké ũnyĩ be ambamba 'dĩrị, ĩri adri 'bávé rụ́'bá ũdrí tị́nị ọfụụ́pi ọfụ ọfụ rĩ agá, 'dĩri lũ kínĩ ngá múké ũnyĩ be ambamba 'dĩri vé ũkpõ íbí íngá Múngú vúgá, adri ' yozú kínĩ, íbí íngá 'bá vúgá kuyé.

2 Kõrínítõ 4:7
(2 Corinthians 4:7 in Keliko)

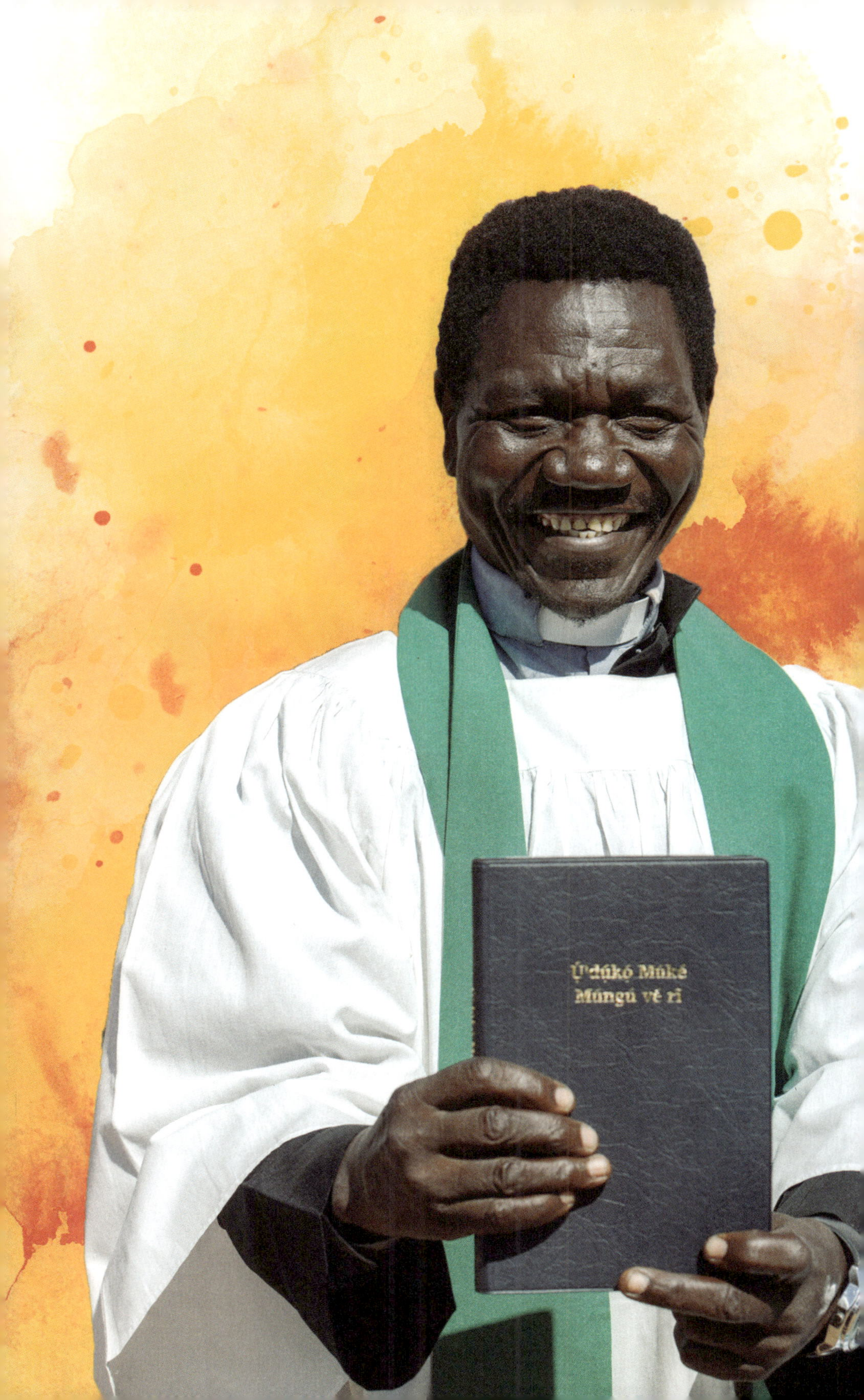
Ụ̃'dụ́kọ́ Múkè
Múngú vé ri

DAY 27

THE ESSENCE OF BAYANIHAN

The goal is for all of them to become one heart and mind—just as you, Father, are in me and I in you, so they might be one heart and mind with us. . . . So they'll be as unified and together as we are—I in them and you in me. Then they'll be mature in this oneness, and give the godless world evidence that you've sent me and loved them in the same way you've loved me.
—John 17:20b-23 (MSG)

When we served in the Philippines, one of the things we learned early on was the value of *bayanihan* (pronounced buy-uh-NEE-hahn). Bayanihan is a core essence of Filipino culture and refers to the spirit of unity, work, and communal cooperation to achieve a particular goal.

In the Philippines, the practice of bayanihan originated with house moving. When we think of moving, we think of packing our belongings into boxes, putting those boxes into cars or trucks and moving to a new place of residence. But in the rural Philippines, houses were made of lightweight indigenous materials like bamboo and coconut leaves. So moving literally meant moving a house. When a family wanted to move, they'd ask men of the town to come help. On the day of the move, fifteen to twenty men would surround the bamboo house, pick it up in unison, and carry the house to the new location. Afterward, the family would express their gratitude by preparing food for everyone to share.

That same spirit is part of everyday conversation for Filipinos. Whenever either of us engaged in one-on-one conversations, we'd answer with independent pronouns like "I" and "my." We quickly learned this was a very Western perspective. Filipinos use inclusive pronouns like "we," "our," and "us," even when they speak one-on-one. This flows from bayanihan.

Every culture has richness, truth, and elements that reflect our Creator. For us, bayanihan reflects the spirit of unity that God desires for his children. It's a reminder that the interdependence of "we" has a far greater impact than the individualistic "me."

Unity is foundational in our call to love one another with one heart, mind, and purpose. But "unity" is a word that's often misunderstood. Some people consider unity to mean oneness that results in being the same, while others think it means the absence of diversity. Scripture, however, paints a different picture of unity.

Unity is not a call to sameness; it's a call to share the same purpose, goal, or vision. The Bible's definition of unity is "to be united most closely (in will and spirit)." As followers of Jesus, our overarching purpose is to love God and people. Our love for God and one another unifies us in Christ and declares the transforming power of his love to the world.

Although unity calls for individuals to come together as one, the end result to unity isn't a group of individuals living individualistic lives; it's an entirely new paradigm. Much like bayanihan has shaped Filipino culture, our unity in Christ shapes us. We can choose to be individuals who come together with the shared goal of seeing Christ proclaimed and lives changed through the translated Word.

SOWING SEEDS

What would it look like for you to practice the essence of bayanihan (unity, work, and communal cooperation) in your own life and community? How can you strive to live in unity with others in a world that so often wants to divide us?

DAY 28

WAITING FOR GOD

I wait for the Lord, my whole being waits,
and in his Word I put my hope.
—Psalm 130:5 (NIV)

Do you remember waiting for something as a kid and thinking it was taking forever for the appointed time to arrive? Waiting for a birthday or Christmas could feel excruciating, yet we knew how long we'd have to wait before these days would come around since they are a designated point in time each year.

But what if you were waiting for something that wasn't a fixed point of time? What if it was an arbitrary event, with nothing concrete to count down to?

That's what it's like for thousands of communities around the world as they wait for Scripture in their own language. And in the fall of 2021, we had the chance to celebrate with one such community—the American Deaf community.

One of our friends and colleagues, Adan Burke, is a native American Sign Language (ASL) user. Adan was born to a hearing family. They tried to figure out how to teach him about Jesus, but they didn't really use ASL.

At three years old, Adan's parents took him to a Deaf church. He learned whatever the Deaf pastors would teach—pastors who would try their best to sign "broken" American Sign Language from reading the English Bible, as Adan described it. As a result, Adan would often miss the point on what the Scripture was about.

During Adan's college days, the Bible began to be accessible in bits and pieces—but on VHS, as that was the medium used at that time. It was the only option, and it was difficult to access because there would be rows and rows of VHS tapes in order to hold the Scriptures. You couldn't carry it with you; it sat on the shelf and took up space.

Then in the early 2010s, Adan became part of a sign language translation project to help make the Bible accessible in ASL. And in 2020, the complete ASLV (American Sign Language Version) Bible was finalized!

Today, Deaf churches in America now have access to the complete Bible in ASL, and transformation is beginning! Adan is witnessing pastors and Deaf leaders stepping up and raising up others to serve the Deaf community and bring them to Christ because the ASLV Bible is finally available for them.

At the time of the completion of the ASLV Bible, Adan was thirty-nine years old; the translation took thirty-eight years. It took his entire lifetime to have the Bible in his own language! But praise God that today, Adan and hundreds of thousands of other ASL users now have access to God's Word in a language and format they can clearly understand.

At Wycliffe's Fall 2021 Scripture Celebration, Adan taught us Psalm 130:5 in ASL. This verse says, "I wait for the Lord, my whole being waits, and in his Word I put my hope." Can you imagine waiting your entire lifetime to meet Jesus in your own language? Praise God that we are able to rejoice with Adan and the ASL community that their wait is finally over!

SOWING SEEDS

Visit **deaf.bible** to watch Psalm 130:5 in ASL. Praise God that the ASL community now has access to their source of hope—Scripture in a format they can clearly understand.

matthews

DAY 29

YEARS OF FAITHFULNESS

But blessed are those who trust in the Lord and have made the Lord their hope and confidence. They are like trees planted along a riverbank, with roots that reach deep into the water. Such trees are not bothered by the heat or worried by long months of drought. Their leaves stay green, and they never stop producing fruit.
—Jeremiah 17:7-8

Nard Pugyao has been our friend for more than twenty years. Nard is Filipino, and the Philippines is actually the first country in Asia that Wycliffe Bible Translators worked in. Because of this, Nard is in many ways one of the "heroes of the faith" in Wycliffe. And once you read his story, you'll know why.

In 1956, Wycliffe Bible translator Dick Roe arrived in Nard's mountain village of Dibagat. Nard watched Dick learn his Isnag language and begin to translate the Gospel of Mark.

Curious about a God who had power over the spirit world, Nard began to study the booklet. He was shocked to read about an all-powerful God who allowed his son to be killed. Nard shook his fist at God and demanded to know why he hadn't protected his son. God answered him, "Nard, I did that for you."

Reading the rest of the booklet, Nard encountered a risen Christ who had victory over sin and death, and he gave his heart to Jesus. Before long, Nard felt God's call to Bible translation and aviation. He went to several aviation-training programs in the United States and joined Wycliffe in 1977. A few years prior, the first Filipino Bible translator, Rudy Barlaan, began assisting Dick in translating the New Testament.

After years of service with Wycliffe and aviation training to become a JAARS (Jungle Aviation and Radio Services) pilot and mechanic, Nard's dream was fulfilled on June 24, 1982, when he landed in Dibagat with the first five hundred copies of the Isnag New Testament and placed them in the hands of his people.

But the work didn't end there! Rudy continued translation work with the Old Testament in 2006, and on July 7, 2021—almost forty years after Nard delivered the New Testament and fifty years after Rudy first began translating—the complete Isnag Bible was finished. Praise God!

It has taken nearly seventy years for the Isnag people to receive God's entire Word. Nard watched his community learn about God's amazing love in their own language. He, Rudy, and those involved in the translation work, have remained faithful to God's calling, knowing that generations of people will be transformed as a result. They are truly living out Jeremiah 17:7-8, which says,

> But blessed are those who trust in the Lord and have made the Lord their hope and confidence. They are like trees planted along a riverbank, with roots that reach deep into the water. Such trees are not bothered by the heat or worried by long months of drought. Their leaves stay green, and they never stop producing fruit.

It's a blessing to witness the faithfulness of those who have trusted in the Lord, who have made him their hope and confidence. And the Isnag people aren't keeping this hope and confidence to themselves! They are working in their neighboring communities to start churches and bring awareness of the need for God's Word in a language and format that people can clearly understand.

Nard and Rudy are thrilled to see God expanding his church—in the Philippines and around the world. The transforming power of God's Word is creating a ripple effect, and may it continue to do so for God's glory!

SOWING SEEDS

Nard, Rudy, and the Isnag people are a great example of lives that have been transformed by having God's Word in their own language. But they're also a great example of how to reach other people and communities for God's glory! How can you reach others for God's glory as well?

May maganggam daya tolay nga e APU
ngala ya piyáran da, se pagpiyáran da.
Meárig da kiya káyu nga nemúla ki dappit
awweg, se magpeyag daya gamut na kiya
danum. Akkan malaylay oray nu magkalíka;
nammáw kammala daya adon na, ay se
makabúngabúnga ngala.

Jeremiah 17:7-8 in Isnag

Nard and Dick

DAY 30

CAN'T STOP, WON'T STOP

God decided in advance to adopt us into his own family by bringing us to himself through Jesus Christ. This is what he wanted to do, and it gave him great pleasure.
—Ephesians 1:5

Have you ever been invited by a friend to tag along to a gathering they were invited to? You might feel uncomfortable or awkward unless you're outgoing and extroverted. When you arrive at this gathering, you likely feel out of place. You're in unfamiliar territory and you don't know anyone. Maybe you don't even really feel wanted because you weren't invited.

Being invited to something personally is so meaningful, isn't it? You know for a fact that the host wants you there because they specifically added you to the guest list. They intentionally sent you an invitation. They were eagerly awaiting your response to be a part of their gathering.

The same is true, spiritually, for people all around the world. They don't want to get a secondhand invitation to join God's global family by receiving the invitation from someone else or in a different language; they want to be personally invited by God himself! They need to receive the invitation in their own language so that they can feel welcomed, included, and wanted.

The vision of Wycliffe Bible Translators is for people from every language to understand the Bible and be transformed. Our mission is to serve with the global body of Christ to advance Bible translation and work together so people can encounter God through his Word. We are helping to extend this personal invitation to be part of God's global family in a language and format that people can clearly understand.

When people receive and accept that invitation, their lives are transformed! They realize that they are valued and loved, and that they belong in the family of God. They recognize that they were chosen to be a part of something bigger than themselves!

We can't stop and we won't stop until this is a reality for all people around the world—to be personally invited into God's family, to begin a relationship with him, to start growing in their faith, and to grow deep roots in the knowledge of who he is.

What an honor and a privilege it is for us as followers of Jesus to be part of God's global family and to invite others to join as well. As Ephesians 1:5 declares, "God decided *in advance* to adopt us into his own family by bringing us to himself through Jesus Christ. This is what he wanted to do, and it gave him great pleasure" (emphasis added).

And this is our joyous prayer:

> Thank you, God, for deciding to adopt us into your family through Jesus! Thank you for wanting to bring us into your family. We long to see Revelation 7:9 fulfilled as more and more people become a part of your big, diverse, multiethnic beautiful tapestry that can only be crafted by your perfect design. Thank you for calling each one of us by name and extending the invitation to be part of your family. May

we be a part of declaring that you can't stop, that you won't stop, until people all around the world—from every nation, people, and language—are able to receive their personal invitation into your family for themselves.

SOWING SEEDS

Get involved in extending God's personal invitation to people around the world through the ministry of Bible translation! You can join a special community of people who are investing in a world where everyone has God's Word in a language and format they clearly understand. How might you help further God's global Kingdom today?

Learn more about Wycliffe, Bible translation, and the inspirational stories of those who have been transformed by God's Word at **wycliffe.org**.

OUR VISION

For people from every language to
understand the Bible and be transformed.

OUR MISSION

Serve with the global body of Christ to advance
Bible translation and work together so people can
encounter God through his Word.

MEET DR. JOHN & KELLY CHESNUT

John serves as President and Chief Executive Officer of Wycliffe Bible Translators USA. Kelly serves as director of spiritual development. John and Kelly, are passionate about seeing God transform people and communities when they experience his Word in a language and format they truly understand.

They spent nine years in the Philippines where John served in a variety of leadership roles with SIL Philippines and SIL International, and Kelly served by leading prayer and spiritual development.

In 2011, the Chesnuts returned to the United States where John served as Chief Development and Partnerships Officer for Wycliffe USA and Kelly continued in prayer ministries. Prior to joining Wycliffe, John and Kelly served in the pastorate for thirteen years. John earned his master of divinity and doctor of ministry from Denver Seminary. Kelly is currently earning her master's degree in global leadership.

John and Kelly have seven children through birth and adoption. They love the tapestry of nations God has woven together in their family. In his spare time, John enjoys the outdoors—whether hiking, teaching his grandkids how to fish, or going on an early morning walk. Kelly loves snuggling with her grandchildren, reading a good book, and sampling chocolate—in just about any form.

KHORYENKOM
KARYEHTANÁ

Ú'dúkó Múké
Múngú vé rĩ

VISIT US

wycliffe.org

CONNECT

@wycliffeusa

SAY HELLO

info@wycliffe.org

PHOTO CREDITS

PAGE 9, *MARC EWELL*

PAGE 17, *EDOUARD TAMBA*

PAGE 25, *WYCLIFFE BIBLE TRANSLATORS*

PAGE 35, *WYCLIFFE BIBLE TRANSLATORS*

PAGE 39, *MATT ARTZ*

PAGE 43, *MARC EWELL*

PAGES 52-53, *MARC EWELL*

PAGES 60-61, *VIKA CHARTIER*

PAGE 65, *WYCLIFFE BIBLE TRANSLATORS*

PAGE 71, *CHRISTINE JESKE*

PAGE 79, *THE JESUS FILM PROJECT*

PAGE 87, *ELAINE BOMBAY*

PAGE 93, *LISA VANDEN BERG*

PAGE 101, *MARC EWELL*

PAGE 109, *DEAF MISSIONS*

PAGE 113, *WYCLIFFE BIBLE TRANSLATORS*

PAGES 120-121, *ELYSE PATTEN, MARC EWELL*

PAGE 124, *AILEEN AGONCILLO*

Wycliffe® Bible Translators